IV. CHURCH SUNDAY SCHOOL: SUNDAY, SEPTEMBER 17, 1995
LESSON: "Phillip: Witness to Outcasts"
SCRIPTURE: Acts 3:4-40

V. CHILDREN'S CHURCH: SUNDAY, OCTOBER 8, 1995
SUBJECT: "God Demonstrates His Love For Us"
SCRIPTURES: Psalm 62:8
LEAD TEACHER: Sis. Vicki Hicks
TEACHERS: Sis. Brenda Whetstone, Bobbie Shaw, & Sheila Marsh
ALTERNATE: Sis. Frazella Pindar
ASSISTANTS: D. Whaley, J. Brooks, S. Gallman & Alisa Brewer

VI. MEMBERSHIP CLASS: OCTOBER 8, 1995 @ 9:30 A.M.
LESSON I: Stewardship & You
LESSON II: Membership & Ministry

CHILDREN LEARN WHAT THEY LIVE

If a child lives with criticism, He learns to condemn
If a child lives with hostility, He learns to fight
If a child lives with ridicule, He learns to be shy
If a child lives with shame, He learns to be guilty
If a child lives with tolerance, He learns to be patient
If a child lives with encouragement, He learns confidence
If a child lives with praise, He learns to appreciate
If a child lives with fairness, He learns justice
If a child lives with security, He learns to have faith
If a child lives with acceptance and friendship
He learns to find love in the world

The Tithe

God has provided His plan for financing the Lord's work and blessing those who will covenant with Him.

> "Bring ye all the tithes into the store house, that there may be meat in mine house, and prove me now herewith, saith the Lord of hosts, if I will not open you the windows of heaven, and pour you out a blessing, that *there shall not be room enough to receive it.*"
> Malachi 3:10

> "Give, and it shall be given unto you; good measure, pressed down, and shaken together, and running over, shall men give into your bosom. For with the same measure that you mete (allot) withal it shall be measured to you agian."
> Luke 6:30

You may give your tithes on a weekly or monthly basis. Either is appropriate. Also, some persons covenant with Lord and <u>bring their tithes current</u> during the *tax refund season* or *Tax Reduction Sunday-* the last Sunday in the calendar year or your firm's fiscal year.

The Tithe is 10% of your net income. For the individual, it is 10% of your income after taxes have been withheld. Subsequently, 10% of one's tax refund is to be tithed- unless you are tithing from your gross income during the year. Examples of financial tithing are as follows:

Monthly Net Income	Your Monthly Tithe
$100.00	$10.00
250.00	25.00
500.00	50.00
1000.00	100.00
2000.00	200.00
3000.00	300.00
4000.00	400.00
5000.00	500.00
10,000.00	1000.00

Once we give our tithes, which is what is <u>**owed**</u> to the Lord, we enter into the realm of giving an offering. The faithfulness of God assures us of the blessing in tithing.

ego-tripping

ego-tripping
and other poems
for young people

nikki giovanni

illustrations by george ford
foreword by virginia hamilton

LAWRENCE HILL BOOKS

library of congress cataloging-in-publication data

Giovanni, Nikki.
    Ego-tripping and other poems for young people / by Nikki Giovanni
  ; with illustrations by George Ford ; foreword by Virginia Hamilton.
  — 2nd ed.
        p.   cm.
    Summary: Thirty-two poems that reflect aspects of the African
American experience.
    ISBN 1-55652-188-X (cloth) : $14.95. — ISBN 1-55652-189-8 (paper)
  : $9.95
    1. Children's poetry, American.   [1. Afro-Americans—Poetry.
2. American poetry—Afro-American authors.]   I. Ford, George
Cephas, ill.   II. Title.
PS3557.I55E4   1993
811'.54—dc20   93-29578
                                                                      CIP
                                                                       AC

poems copyright 1973, 1993 by nikki giovanni
illustrations copyright 1973, 1993 by george ford
foreword copyright 1993 by virginia hamilton
all rights reserved
permission to reprint the following poems:
alone, kidnap poem, the genie in the jar, 2nd rapp,
ego-tripping, poem for flora, poem for my nephew
has been granted by broadside press, detroit, michigan.

permission to reprint the following poems:
black power, word poem, poem for black boys, the
funeral of martin luther king, jr., nikki-rosa,
intellectualism, knoxville, tennessee has been granted
by william morrow & company, inc., new york, new york.

printed in mexico
second edition
published by lawrence hill books, new york, new york
an imprint of chicago review press, incorporated
814 north franklin st.
chicago, illinois 60610

contents

foreword

She's a professional writer and a college professor who cares about uses of art and uses of her work. She's a renowned poet who, by utilizing startling imagery uniquely her own, attempts to open young people's minds—to connect herself with them and connect them to living.

She writes in a colloquial language that is seemingly artless. But that, of course, is its artistry. It is a workable style without guile or pretension; and yet the clean poetry of it is pointed and directed to the head and heart, as in "a poem (for langston hughes)":

> diamonds are mined . . . oil is discovered
> gold is found . . . but thoughts are uncovered
>
> wool is sheared . . . silk is spun
> weaving is hard . . . but words are fun

I'm talking about my poet-friend Nikki Giovanni. She has always been very human and open with me. In this new and expanded collection of her book *ego-tripping and other poems for young people*, first published in 1973, she be the same to all the young ones listening and reading. Her voice is personal and warm, even when she be sounding like the griot, the storyteller, passing along how it was to grow up black and revolutionary in the sixties.

That's when I first met Nikki, in New York. As a young, activist poet, she was interested in my first novel, *Zeely*, and she used it as a play to speak directly to young people about their African American heritage. She was working with young people, actors, touring with them performing the "Zeely" play.

She and I share a bit of the geography of southwestern Ohio. I was born there and she came to live in Cincinnati. But no one place could hold Giovanni for long. In the seventies and eighties, she was always on the road, constantly searching in her enthusiasm for the young. It was as though she feared if she bought a bed, she'd have to put it somewhere and lie in it. She'd have to build a house around it and live in rooms. Instead, she lectured everywhere, taught anybody who was ready to read and listen. She was, indeed, the Princess of Black Poetry. And her poetry readings, packed with young and old alike, were astounding rhythms of her voice seeing into life and into us who lived it, looking us in the eye, as in "poem for my nephew":

> i wish i were
> a shadow
> oh wow! when they put
> the light on
> me i'd grow
> longer and taller and
> BLACKER

Even though Nikki Giovanni is based in a university now, she still travels America when she is free. She still gets out the word.

I was born several years before her, and yet we share identical symbols. Cultural icons span our generation, and black cultural threads weave intact between us. Both of us use the same raw materials of human relationships to shape our language.

Giovanni with her poetry celebrates ordinary folks. Her creations are manuals for survival. She gives young people tools to help them prevail in an America that can be overpoweringly hostile and indifferent to them.

In "poem for two jameses (ballantine and snow in iron cells)," she writes:

we all start
as a speck
nobody notices us
but some may hope
we're there
some count days and wait

we grow
in a cell that spreads
like a summer cold
to other people . . .

they put us in a cell
to make us behave
never realizing it's from cells
we have escaped
and we will be born
from their iron cells
new people with a new cry

In Giovanni's *ego-tripping*, young people are taught how to live, to know, and to remember who they are. There is deliverance for them in these poems of struggle and liberation. In her vivid words, young people be made to feel what life is. They weep, their hearts are touched. They laugh, they are loved and made strong. They are reborn. Good that there is Giovanni here for them; best that she be among us all, writing the images and sounding the meter and verse of a better world.

Virginia Hamilton
Yellow Springs, Ohio
September 1993

part one

"I am the Lorax. I speak for the trees.
I speak for the trees, for the trees have no tongues."
—Dr. Seuss

a poem
(for langston hughes)

diamonds are mined ... oil is discovered
gold is found ... but thoughts are uncovered

wool is sheared ... silk is spun
weaving is hard ... but words are fun

highways span ... bridges connect
country roads ramble ... but i suspect

    if i took a rainbow ride
    i could be there by your side

metaphor has its point of view
allusions and illusion ... too

meter ... verse ... classical ... free
poems are what you do to me

let's look at it one more time
since i've put this rap in rhyme

    when i take my rainbow ride
    you'll be right there at my side

hey bop hey bop hey re re bop

ego-tripping
(there may be a reason why)

I was born in the congo
I walked to the fertile crescent and built
   the sphinx
I designed a pyramid so tough that a star
    that only glows every one hundred years falls
    into the center giving divine perfect light
I am bad

I sat on the throne
   drinking nectar with allah
I got hot and sent an ice age to europe
   to cool my thirst
My oldest daughter is nefertiti
   the tears from my birth pains
   created the nile
I am a beautiful woman

I gazed on the forest and burned
    out the sahara desert
    with a packet of goat's meat
    and a change of clothes
I crossed it in two hours
I am a gazelle so swift
    so swift you can't catch me

    For a birthday present when he was three
I gave my son hannibal an elephant
    He gave me rome for mother's day
My strength flows ever on

My son noah built new/ark and
I stood proudly at the helm
    as we sailed on a soft summer day

I turned myself into myself and was
    jesus
    men intone my loving name

    All praises All praises
I am the one who would save

I sowed diamonds in my back yard
My bowels deliver uranium
    the filings from my fingernails are
    semi-precious jewels
    On a trip north
I caught a cold and blew
My nose giving oil to the arab world
I am so hip even my errors are correct
I sailed west to reach east and had to round off
    the earth as I went
    The hair from my head thinned and gold was
    laid across three continents

I am so perfect so divine so ethereal so surreal
I cannot be comprehended
    except by my permission

I mean...I...can fly
    like a bird in the sky...

poem for two jameses
(ballantine and snow
in iron cells)

we all start
as a speck
nobody notices us
but some may hope
we're there
some count days and wait

we grow
in a cell that spreads
like a summer cold
to other people
they notice and laugh
some are happy
some wish to stop
our movement

we kick and move
are stubborn and demanding
completely inside
the system

they put us in a cell
to make us behave
never realizing it's from cells
we have escaped
and we will be born
from their iron cells
new people with a new cry

poem for lloyd

it's a drag
sitting around waiting
for death
gotta do something before
i die

it's so lonely dying
all alone
gotta do something
before i die
gotta gotta get a gun
walking talking thinking gun
before i die

they're so lonely
funeral dirges
hip black angry funeral
dirges
gotta gotta get a gun
it's so lonely
when you die
gotta gotta get a gun to kill
death

for the masai warriors

(of don miller)

remembering my father's drum
remembering the leopard's screech
if i could weave an ancient rope
and tie myself to history
i'd spring like daylight out of night
into the future of our land
i'd sprint across the grassy plain
and make a nation for the gods
where i could be the man

word poem
(perhaps worth considering)

as things be/come
let's destroy
then we can destroy
what we be/come
let's build
what we become
when we dream

the funeral of
martin luther king, jr.

His headstone said
FREE AT LAST, FREE AT LAST
But death is a slave's freedom
We seek the freedom of free men
And the construction of a world
Where Martin Luther King could have lived
and preached non-violence

no reservations

(for art jones)

there are no reservations
for the revolution

no polite little clerk
to send notice
to your room
saying you are WANTED
on the battlefield

there are no banners
to wave you forward
no blaring trumpets
not even a blues note
moaning wailing lone blue note
to the yoruba drums saying
strike now   shoot
strike now   fire
strike now   run

there will be no grand
parade
and a lot thrown round
your neck
people won't look up and say
"why he used to live next to me
isn't it nice
it's his turn now"

there will be no recruitment
station
where you can give
the most convenient hours
"monday wednesday i play ball
friday night i play cards
any other time i'm free"

there will be no reserve
of energy
no slacking off till next time
"let's see—i can come back
next week
better not wear myself out
this time"

there will be reservations
only
if we fail

revolutionary music

you've just got to dig sly
and the family stone
forget the words
you gonna be dancing to the music
james brown can go to
viet nam
or sing about whatever he
has to
since he already told
the honkie
"although you happy you better try
to get along
money won't change you
but time is taking you on"
not to mention
doing a whole
song they can't even snap
their fingers to
"good god! ugh!"
talking bout
"i got the feeling baby i got the feeling"
and "hey everybody let me tell you the news"
martha and the vandellas dancing in the streets
while shorty long is functioning at that junction
yeah we hip to that

aretha said they better
think
but she already said
"ain't no way to love you"
(and you know she wasn't talking to us)
and dig the o'jays asking "must i always be a stand
in for love"
i mean they say "i'm a fool for being myself"

While the mighty mighty impressions have told the
world
for once and for all
"We're a Winner"
even our names—le roi has said—are together
impressions
temptations
supremes
delfonics
miracles
intruders (i mean intruders?)
not beatles and animals and white bad things like
young rascals and shit
we be digging all
our revolutionary music consciously or un
cause sam cooke said "a change is gonna come"

poem for my nephew
(brother c. b. soul)

i wish i were
a shadow
oh wow! when they put
the light on
me i'd grow
longer and taller and
BLACKER

intellectualism

sometimes i feel like i just get in
everybody's way
when i was a little girl
i used to go read
or make fudge
when i got bigger i
read
or picked my nose
that's what they called
intelligence
or when i got older
intellectualism
but it was only
that i was in the way

black power
(for all the beautiful
black panthers east)

But the whole thing is a miracle—See?

We were just standing there
talking—not touching or smoking
Pot
When this cop told
Tyrone
Move along buddy—take your whores
outa here

And this tremendous growl
From out of nowhere
Pounced on him

Nobody to this very day
Can explain
How it happened

And none of the zoos or circuses
Within fifty miles
Had reported
A panther
Missing

the genie in the jar
(for nina simone)

take a note and spin it around spin it around don't
prick your finger
take a note and spin it around
on the Black loom on the Black loom
careful baby
don't prick your finger

take the air and weave the sky
around the Black loom around the Black loom
make the sky sing a Black song sing a blue song
sing my song make the sky sing a Black song
from the Black loom from the Black loom
careful baby
don't prick your finger

take the genie and put her in a jar
put her in a jar
wrap the sky around her
take the genie and put her in a jar
wrap the sky around her
listen to her sing
sing a Black song our Black song
from the Black loom
singing to me
from the Black loom
careful baby
don't prick your finger

poem for flora

when she was little
and colored and ugly with short
straightened hair
and a very pretty smile
she went to sunday school to hear
'bout nebuchadnezzar the king
of the jews

and she would listen

shadrach, meshach and abednego in the fire

and she would learn

how god was neither north
nor south east or west
with no color but all
she remembered was that
Sheba was Black and comely

and she would think

i want to be
like that

beautiful black men
(with compliments and apologies
to all not mentioned by name)

i wanta say just gotta say something
bout those beautiful beautiful beautiful outasight
black men
with they afros
walking down the street
is the same ol danger
but a brand new pleasure

sitting on stoops, in bars, going to offices
running numbers, watching for their whores
preaching in churches, driving their hogs
walking their dogs, winking at me
in their fire red, lime green, burnt orange
royal blue tight tight pants that hug
what i like to hug

jerry butler, wilson pickett, the impressions
temptations, mighty mighty sly
don't have to do anything but walk
on stage
and i scream and stamp and shout
see new breed men in breed alls
dashiki suits with shirts that match
the lining that complements the ties
that smile at the sandals
where dirty toes peek at me
and i scream and stamp and shout
for more beautiful beautiful beautiful
black men with outasight afros

poem for black boys
(with special love to james)

Where are your heroes, my little Black ones
You are the Indian you so disdainfully shoot
Not the big bad sheriff on his faggoty white horse

You should play run-away-slave
or Mau Mau
These are more in line with your history

Ask your mothers for a Rap Brown gun
Santa just may comply if you wish hard enough
Ask for CULLURD instead of Monopoly
DO NOT SIT IN DO NOT FOLLOW KING
GO DIRECTLY TO STREETS
This is a game you can win

As you sit there with your all understanding eyes
You know the truth of what I'm saying
Play Back-to-Black
Grow a natural and practice vandalism
These are useful games (some say a skill is even
learned)

There is a new game I must tell you of
It's called Catch The Leader Lying
(and knowing your sense of the absurd
you will enjoy this)

Also a company called Revolution has just issued
a special kit for little boys
called Burn Baby
I'm told it has full instructions on how to siphon gas
and fill a bottle

Then our old friend Hide and Seek becomes valid
Because we have much to seek and ourselves to hide
from a lecherous dog

And this poem I give is worth much more
than any nickel bag
or ten cent toy
And you will understand all too soon
That you, my children of battle, are your heroes
You must invent your own games and teach us old
ones how to play

part two

"how would you like to go up in the sky?"
—robert louis stevenson

revolutionary dreams

i used to dream militant
dreams of taking
over america to show
these white folks how it should be
done
i used to dream radical dreams
of blowing everyone away with my perceptive
powers
of correct analysis
i even used to think i'd be the one
to stop the riot and negotiate the peace
then i awoke and dug
that if i dreamed natural
dreams of being a natural
woman doing what a woman
does when she's natural
i would have a revolution

the price of patience
(for hilbert on his retirement
as english department head)

There are things ... that should not be touched:
    Books when your hands are sticky with
      chocolate
    Cars when your clothes are covered with oil
    Men when your heart does not love them
Frost is right: Good neighbors make good fences

There is something about the human spirit ... that
cannot be tamed and should not be trained
There is something wild ... in our souls and our
eyes ... that must be free ... to explore the horizon
It is dangerous ... to wake a sleeping tiger
It is foolish ... to ravish a man's pride
Why do we always mistake kindness ... for
weakness

Don't we know the price of patience

Winter always yields to Spring and she concedes
to Summer
It is the natural order of things ... Compromise ...
We construct change ... to bring change ...
to change again
This is only right ... Yet

There are some things ... that should not be touched
Unless we are able ... to adequately replace or
repair them:

    Do Not Shoot the Cacti
    Collect Your Trash at Antarctica
    Do Not Touch a Man ... Unless You Love Him

reading the
backs of books

(for frank tota on his retirement as superintendent of roanoke schools)

I'm not a real mystery reader... I can't handle real
murders... or stalking killers... or reading about
the pain... and humiliation of victims... I have
no interest... in why the killer killed... or how
the victim... was complaisant... Though it is a
deep secret... it is not a dirty one... that I read
the backs of all books... first

One need look... no farther... than my college
major... History... to know I believe... we

divine the future . . . from the past . . . That residing
in us all . . . are the seeds of possibility . . . Heroes
are not born . . . they are made of circumstances
. . . Ordinary people . . . do . . . indeed . . . perform
extraordinary deeds . . . It is only logical

But I would be remiss . . . to assume any helmsman
. . . can bring the ship to shore . . . And though we
look . . . for ports in storms . . . we prefer safe
harbors . . . and calming . . . welcoming . . . waters

I cannot know this ending . . . but I know this history
. . . Frank Tota is a prime helmsman . . . who has
steered our future . . . to a better point . . . He has
sailed forth . . . in troubled waters . . . and seen
the ship . . . put in . . . We have learned . . . from
his patience and impatience . . . that we are a better
crew . . . than before . . . We have learned . . . from
his words and example . . . that we are more
capable than we thought . . .

His presence will be missed . . . but there is no
greater accolade . . . to ascribe to a teacher . . . than
that he has taught

2nd rapp

they ain't gonna never get
rap
he's a note turned himself
into a million songs listen
to aretha call
his name

he's a light
turned himself into our homes
look how well we see
since he came

he's a spirit turned
pisces to aries
alpha to omega

he's a man
turned himself into Black
women
and we turn little hims
loose on the world

a poem for carol
(may she always wear red ribbons)

when i was very little
though it's still true today
there were no sidewalks in lincoln heights
and the home we had on jackson street
was right next to a bus stop and a sewer
which didn't really ever become offensive
but one day from the sewer a little kitten
with one eye gone
came crawling out
though she never really came into our yard but just
sort of hung by to watch the folk
my sister who was always softhearted but able
to act effectively started taking milk
out to her while our father would only say
don't bring *him* home and everyday
after school i would rush home to see if she was still
there and if gary had fed her but i could never
bring myself to go near her
she was so loving
and so hurt and so singularly beautiful and i knew
i had nothing to give that would
replace her one gone eye

and if i had named her which i didn't i'm sure
i would have called her carol

knoxville, tennessee

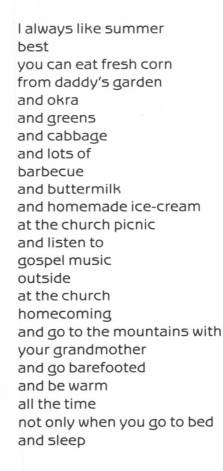

I always like summer
best
you can eat fresh corn
from daddy's garden
and okra
and greens
and cabbage
and lots of
barbecue
and buttermilk
and homemade ice-cream
at the church picnic
and listen to
gospel music
outside
at the church
homecoming
and go to the mountains with
your grandmother
and go barefooted
and be warm
all the time
not only when you go to bed
and sleep

november

snowflakes waltz around my ears
i twirl in rhythm to the dance
of peppermint dreams
and mistletoe

kissing you

snowflakes ballet in my heart
warming me to crystal dreams
of dancing to that midnight sun

kissing you

snowflakes laugh and go away
taking dance and crystal dreams
leaving me   alone with you
to falalalalalalala

kidnap poem

ever been kidnapped
by a poet
if i were a poet
i'd kidnap you
put you in my phrases and meter
you to jones beach
or maybe coney island
or maybe just to my house
lyric you in lilacs
dash you in the rain
blend into the beach
to complement my see
play the lyre for you
ode you with my love song
anything to win you
wrap you in the red Black green
show you off to mama
yeah if i were a poet i'd kid
nap you

dreams

in my younger years
before i learned
black people aren't
suppose to dream
i wanted to be
a raelet
and say "dr o wn d in my youn tears"
or "tal kin bout tal kin bout"
or be marjorie hendricks and grind
all up against the mic
and scream
"baaaaaby nightandday
baaaaaby nightandday"
then as i grew and matured
i became more sensible
and decided i would
settle down
and just become
a sweet inspiration

communication

if music is the universal language
think of me as one whole note

if science has the most perfect language
imagine me as Mc^2

since mathematics can speak to the infinite
picture me as 1 to the first power

what i mean is one day
i'm gonna grab your love

and you'll be satisfied

alone

i can be
alone by myself
i was
lonely alone
now i'm lonely
with you
something is wrong
there are flies
everywhere
i go

everytime it rains

everytime it rains if it's summer
the sky turns pink and the earth smelling
very sweaty calls my feet to play

i usually sit in my chrome kitchen chair
trying to figure how many worms
were drowned and why i didn't for once
go outside naked
    i want to learn
    how to laugh

once i had three plaits and three ribbons
and blue and white seersucker pants
and a lace tee shirt
i grabbed a bunch of grapes and went to find
the end of a rainbow

i walked through the park
up the hill past the vacant lot they just tore down
past the newsstand and the pool hall and still
wasn't there

i remember sitting on the curb in the drizzle

that was funny
but i still didn't laugh

nikki-rosa

childhood remembrances are always a drag
if you're Black
you always remember things like living in Woodlawn
with no inside toilet
and if you become famous or something
they never talk about how happy you were to have
your mother
all to yourself and
how good the water felt when you got your bath
from one of those
big tubs that folk in chicago barbecue in
and somehow when you talk about home
it never gets across how much you
understood their feelings
as the whole family attended meetings about
Hollydale
and even though you remember
your biographers never understand
your father's pain as he sells his stock
and another dream goes
And though you're poor it isn't poverty that
concerns you
and though they fought a lot
it isn't your father's drinking that makes any
difference
but only that everybody is together and you
and your sister have happy birthdays and very good
Christmases

and I really hope no white person ever has cause
to write about me
because they never understand
Black love is Black wealth and they'll
probably talk about my hard childhood
and never understand that
all the while I was quite happy

the flowering
of change
(the inaugural of toni iadoralo)

What would May flowers be...if March winds and
April showers
Combine...not just the tulips of Spring
          nor the first peeks of crabgrass
          growing
But the idea...that opposite needs...satisfy the
universal
Compulsion...to awaken the dormant seeds of
newness
Forcing the damp cold muddy foundation to accept
The flowering ...of Change

It's funny...that Change is something we get...
when we give
Something...solid...One needs:
    Exact Change...to board a bus or make a
             societal Contribution
At checkout lines...one hopes for
    Even Change...so that
    Little Change...doesn't weight our pockets
          down
Sometimes the weight of
    Change causes us to Change:
     Our clothes
     Where we keep our treasures
     How we think...about
     Change
    Change is a way...of experiencing

A great mind once said "Experience is a good teacher though
A fool will have none other" He spoke to reluctant Change...that
Change that only necessity brings...that Change compelled by
Fire...or wind...or flood...Instead of love...
foresight...compassion...It may well be that we only Change...when we
Must...But we Must...learn...to Change
...before we have...to

One Change we celebrate...is when the new year
(diapers and Arrows) moves old man time...
away...
Bells ring...whistles
Blow...strangers embrace...and wish us happiness...But January
Is only a calendar Change...and there are many others:
    We congratulate couples who Changed into
      one family
    We praise institutions...governments...
      attitudes which Change the course of
      human events
    We mourn death while celebrating the life that
      was
Everything will Change...because all is living
These steps we take:
    To walk
    To run
    To fly
These leaps we take:
    Of hope
    Of trust
    Of belief

Are affirmations to our commitment:
    To life
    To living
    Today we celebrate...A Change...Knowing fields will
Once again need plowing...Seeds will once again need planting...
Rain and sun will once again...have to come... before we once
Again experience the goodness

Graduations...Installations...Plowing... Planting...Waiting
For a Change to come...Waiting for a Change... to come...Waiting
For a Change

racing against the sun

I ride the rainbow...spinning around
blending...bending...down through the stars
winding my way...to the ocean of Dreams
    Racing against the sun

There isn't much time...I have so much to do
I forge westward Ho with a dream or two
for all the boys and girls warm in their beds
    Waiting for the sun

I'm like the wind...I can't be seen
Whispering through...on the dust of moonbeams
I blanket the world...with peppermint dreams
    Home before the sun

foundation-wise:
rock solid

I am archaeology... I mine the human soul... for
undiscovered strength

I am history... I search our past... for
unacknowledged truths

I am a raindrop... determined to make a Grand
Canyon

I am a rock... charged by the spirit of humanity
... to rise to mountainous proportions

I am the salve... Liberally, Artfully, Scientifically
... apply me

I come to satisfy... I am a poem

Rocks are not born... they are made... fused
from sand and sea
Boiled to a fine volcanic brew... till liquefied...
they bubble over... laughingly reaching... for
the sun
Finding instead... a cold north wind...
stopping the sun dance... with jagged edges

What good is a butterfly

I am a moth...flirting dangerously with light...
my season is not long

I am life...holding in my tenuous hand...All that
humans ever will know

Butterflies...and books...last forever